50 Beef Lunch Meals

By: Kelly Johnson

Table of Contents

- Classic Beef Tacos
- Beef and Broccoli Stir-Fry
- Philly Cheesesteak Sandwich
- Beef and Bean Chili
- Korean Bulgogi Bowls
- Spaghetti with Beef Bolognese
- Beef Stroganoff Pasta
- Beef Burrito Bowls
- BBQ Beef Sliders
- Beef and Vegetable Soup
- Grilled Beef Kabobs
- Beef and Cheddar Wraps
- Thai Beef Salad
- Beef Enchiladas
- Beef and Mushroom Risotto
- Teriyaki Beef Stir-Fry
- Shepherd's Pie
- Beef Potstickers
- Beef Nachos Supreme
- Beef Quesadillas
- Slow-Cooked Beef Ragu
- Beef and Sweet Potato Hash
- Chipotle Beef Tacos
- Beef Wellington Bites
- Beef Meatball Subs
- Chimichurri Steak Salad
- Beef Stuffed Bell Peppers
- Moroccan Spiced Beef Stew
- Beef Lasagna Rolls
- Beef Curry with Rice
- Roast Beef Sandwiches
- Beef and Spinach Quiche
- Beef Lettuce Wraps
- Mongolian Beef with Rice
- Beef and Cheese Empanadas

- Shredded Beef Tostadas
- Beef Sloppy Joes
- Beef Pad Thai
- Grilled Steak and Asparagus Salad
- Beef Burrito Enchiladas
- Spicy Beef Stir-Fry with Noodles
- Beef and Black Bean Chili
- Mediterranean Beef Pita Wraps
- Steak Tacos with Lime Crema
- Classic Beef Burger
- Beef and Barley Soup
- Steak and Potato Salad
- Beef Picadillo
- Italian Beef Paninis
- Beef Fried Rice

Classic Beef Tacos

Ingredients

- **For the Beef Filling:**
    - 1 lb (450 g) ground beef
    - 1 medium onion, finely chopped
    - 2 cloves garlic, minced
    - 1 tbsp olive oil
    - 2 tsp chili powder
    - 1 tsp ground cumin
    - 1/2 tsp smoked paprika
    - 1/2 tsp oregano
    - 1/2 tsp salt (or to taste)
    - 1/4 tsp black pepper
    - 1/4 cup tomato sauce (or salsa)
    - 1/4 cup beef or chicken broth
- **For the Tacos:**
    - 8 small corn or flour tortillas
    - 1 cup shredded lettuce
    - 1 cup shredded cheddar or Mexican cheese blend
    - 1 medium tomato, diced
    - 1/2 cup sour cream
    - 1/2 cup guacamole (optional)
    - 1/4 cup chopped fresh cilantro
    - Lime wedges, for serving

Instructions

1. Heat olive oil in a large skillet over medium heat. Add chopped onion and sauté for 2-3 minutes until softened.
2. Stir in minced garlic and cook for 30 seconds until fragrant.
3. Add ground beef to the skillet. Cook and break it up with a spatula until browned and no longer pink (about 5-7 minutes).
4. Drain any excess fat if necessary, then stir in chili powder, cumin, smoked paprika, oregano, salt, and pepper.
5. Mix in tomato sauce and broth. Let it simmer for 3-4 minutes, stirring occasionally, until the mixture thickens slightly. Remove from heat.
6. Heat tortillas in a dry skillet over medium heat for 30 seconds per side or wrap them in foil and warm them in the oven at 350°F (175°C) for 5 minutes.

7. Place a spoonful of beef filling onto each tortilla. Add shredded lettuce, cheese, diced tomato, and any additional toppings such as sour cream, guacamole, or cilantro.
8. Serve immediately with lime wedges on the side.

Beef and Broccoli Stir-Fry

Ingredients

- 1 lb (450 g) beef sirloin or flank steak, thinly sliced
- 3 cups broccoli florets
- 2 tbsp vegetable oil
- 3 cloves garlic, minced
- 1 tbsp ginger, minced
- 1/4 cup soy sauce
- 2 tbsp oyster sauce
- 1 tbsp cornstarch mixed with 2 tbsp water
- 1 tbsp brown sugar
- 1/4 tsp black pepper

Instructions

1. Heat 1 tbsp of oil in a large skillet or wok over high heat. Stir-fry the beef for 2-3 minutes until browned. Remove and set aside.
2. Add the remaining oil to the pan and stir-fry the broccoli for 3-4 minutes until crisp-tender.
3. Stir in garlic and ginger, cooking for 30 seconds.
4. Return the beef to the pan. Add soy sauce, oyster sauce, sugar, and pepper. Stir well.
5. Pour in the cornstarch slurry and cook for another 1-2 minutes until the sauce thickens.
6. Serve hot with rice or noodles.

Philly Cheesesteak Sandwich

Ingredients

- 1 lb (450 g) ribeye steak, thinly sliced
- 1 medium onion, thinly sliced
- 1 green bell pepper, thinly sliced
- 8 slices provolone cheese
- 4 hoagie rolls
- 2 tbsp butter
- 2 tbsp vegetable oil
- Salt and black pepper, to taste

Instructions

1. Heat 1 tbsp of oil and 1 tbsp of butter in a skillet over medium heat. Sauté onions and bell peppers until soft and caramelized. Remove and set aside.
2. Heat the remaining oil and butter in the same skillet. Add the sliced steak, season with salt and pepper, and cook until browned.
3. Reduce heat to low, return the onions and peppers, and layer provolone slices over the mixture until melted.
4. Toast hoagie rolls lightly and fill them with the steak mixture.
5. Serve warm and enjoy!

Beef and Bean Chili

Ingredients

- 1 lb (450 g) ground beef
- 1 medium onion, diced
- 3 cloves garlic, minced
- 1 can (15 oz) kidney beans, rinsed and drained
- 1 can (15 oz) diced tomatoes
- 1 tbsp tomato paste
- 2 cups beef broth
- 2 tsp chili powder
- 1 tsp ground cumin
- 1/2 tsp smoked paprika
- 1/2 tsp oregano
- Salt and black pepper, to taste
- Optional toppings: sour cream, shredded cheese, chopped green onions

Instructions

1. In a large pot, cook ground beef over medium heat until browned. Drain excess fat.
2. Add onion and garlic to the pot and sauté for 2-3 minutes until fragrant.
3. Stir in chili powder, cumin, smoked paprika, oregano, salt, and pepper.
4. Add kidney beans, diced tomatoes, tomato paste, and beef broth. Mix well.
5. Bring to a simmer, reduce heat, and let it cook uncovered for 20-25 minutes, stirring occasionally.
6. Serve hot with your favorite toppings.

Korean Bulgogi Bowls

Ingredients

- 1 lb (450 g) thinly sliced beef (ribeye or sirloin)
- 1/4 cup soy sauce
- 2 tbsp brown sugar
- 1 tbsp sesame oil
- 3 cloves garlic, minced
- 1 tbsp grated ginger
- 1/4 tsp black pepper
- 1 medium onion, sliced
- Cooked rice, for serving
- Sliced cucumber, shredded carrots, and green onions for garnish

Instructions

1. Combine soy sauce, sugar, sesame oil, garlic, ginger, and black pepper in a bowl. Add the beef and marinate for 30 minutes.
2. Heat a skillet over medium-high heat and cook the beef with onions until browned and caramelized.
3. Serve over rice with fresh vegetables and garnish.

Spaghetti with Beef Bolognese

Ingredients

- 1 lb (450 g) ground beef
- 1 medium onion, diced
- 2 cloves garlic, minced
- 1 can (15 oz) crushed tomatoes
- 1/4 cup tomato paste
- 1/2 cup beef broth
- 1 tsp oregano
- 1 tsp basil
- Salt and pepper, to taste
- Spaghetti, cooked al dente
- Grated Parmesan cheese, for serving

Instructions

1. In a large skillet, cook beef until browned. Remove excess fat.
2. Add onion and garlic; cook until softened.
3. Stir in crushed tomatoes, tomato paste, broth, and herbs. Simmer for 20 minutes.
4. Toss with spaghetti and serve with Parmesan.

Beef Stroganoff Pasta

Ingredients

- 1 lb (450 g) beef sirloin, thinly sliced
- 1 medium onion, diced
- 1 cup mushrooms, sliced
- 2 cloves garlic, minced
- 1 cup sour cream
- 1 cup beef broth
- 2 tbsp flour
- 2 tbsp butter
- Egg noodles, cooked

Instructions

1. Sauté beef in butter until browned. Remove and set aside.
2. Cook onion, garlic, and mushrooms in the same pan.
3. Stir in flour, then add broth and simmer until thickened.
4. Return beef and stir in sour cream. Serve over egg noodles.

Beef Burrito Bowls

Ingredients

- 1 lb (450 g) ground beef
- 1 packet taco seasoning
- 1 cup cooked rice
- 1 can (15 oz) black beans
- 1 cup salsa
- 1 cup shredded lettuce
- 1 cup shredded cheese
- Sour cream and guacamole for topping

Instructions

1. Cook beef with taco seasoning until browned.
2. Assemble bowls with rice, beans, beef, and toppings.

BBQ Beef Sliders

Ingredients

- 2 cups shredded cooked beef
- 1 cup barbecue sauce
- Slider buns
- Coleslaw for topping

Instructions

1. Mix beef with barbecue sauce and heat through.
2. Serve on slider buns with coleslaw.

Beef and Vegetable Soup

Ingredients

- 1 lb (450 g) beef stew meat
- 2 cups mixed vegetables (carrots, celery, potatoes)
- 1 can (15 oz) diced tomatoes
- 4 cups beef broth
- 1 tsp thyme
- Salt and pepper, to taste

Instructions

1. Brown beef in a large pot. Add vegetables, tomatoes, and broth.
2. Simmer until beef is tender and vegetables are cooked.

Grilled Beef Kabobs

Ingredients

- 1 lb (450 g) beef sirloin, cubed
- 1 bell pepper, cubed
- 1 onion, cubed
- 1/4 cup soy sauce
- 2 tbsp olive oil
- 1 tbsp honey

Instructions

1. Marinate beef in soy sauce, olive oil, and honey for 30 minutes.
2. Thread beef and vegetables onto skewers. Grill until cooked through.

Beef and Cheddar Wraps

Ingredients

- 1 lb (450 g) thinly sliced roast beef
- 4 large tortillas
- 1 cup shredded cheddar cheese
- 1/2 cup mayonnaise
- 1/4 cup horseradish sauce

Instructions

1. Spread mayonnaise and horseradish on tortillas.
2. Add roast beef and cheese. Roll tightly and slice in half.

Thai Beef Salad

Ingredients

- 1 lb (450 g) flank steak, grilled and thinly sliced
- 1 cup mixed salad greens
- 1 cucumber, julienned
- 1/2 red onion, thinly sliced
- 1 carrot, julienned
- 1/4 cup fresh cilantro, chopped
- 2 tbsp fish sauce
- 1 tbsp lime juice
- 1 tbsp sugar
- 1 tbsp soy sauce
- 1 tsp chili flakes (optional)
- 1/4 cup chopped peanuts (for garnish)

Instructions

1. Grill or pan-sear the flank steak until cooked to your liking. Slice thinly against the grain.
2. Toss together greens, cucumber, onion, carrot, and cilantro in a large bowl.
3. In a small bowl, whisk together fish sauce, lime juice, sugar, soy sauce, and chili flakes.
4. Drizzle dressing over the salad and top with sliced beef and chopped peanuts. Serve immediately.

Beef Enchiladas

Ingredients

- 1 lb (450 g) ground beef
- 1 medium onion, diced
- 1 can (10 oz) enchilada sauce
- 8 corn tortillas
- 1 cup shredded cheese (cheddar or Mexican blend)
- 1/2 tsp cumin
- 1/2 tsp chili powder
- Salt and pepper, to taste

Instructions

1. Brown ground beef with onion in a skillet. Add cumin, chili powder, salt, and pepper.
2. Pour a small amount of enchilada sauce into the bottom of a baking dish.
3. Roll up beef mixture in tortillas and place in the dish. Pour remaining enchilada sauce over the top.
4. Sprinkle cheese on top and bake at 375°F (190°C) for 20 minutes, until bubbly and golden.

Beef and Mushroom Risotto

Ingredients

- 1 lb (450 g) beef sirloin, thinly sliced
- 1 cup Arborio rice
- 1/2 lb mushrooms, sliced
- 1 medium onion, diced
- 2 cloves garlic, minced
- 1/4 cup white wine
- 4 cups beef broth
- 1/2 cup Parmesan cheese, grated
- 2 tbsp butter
- Salt and pepper, to taste

Instructions

1. Cook beef in a skillet until browned, then set aside.
2. In the same pan, sauté mushrooms, onion, and garlic until softened.
3. Stir in rice, and cook for 1-2 minutes. Add wine and cook until absorbed.
4. Gradually add broth, stirring constantly, until rice is tender and creamy.
5. Stir in cooked beef, Parmesan cheese, butter, and season with salt and pepper. Serve immediately.

Teriyaki Beef Stir-Fry

Ingredients

- 1 lb (450 g) beef sirloin or flank steak, thinly sliced
- 2 tbsp vegetable oil
- 1 bell pepper, sliced
- 1 carrot, julienned
- 1/2 onion, sliced
- 3 tbsp soy sauce
- 2 tbsp teriyaki sauce
- 1 tbsp sesame oil
- 1 tsp garlic, minced
- 1 tsp ginger, minced
- Cooked rice, for serving

Instructions

1. Heat oil in a large skillet or wok. Cook beef until browned, then set aside.
2. In the same pan, cook vegetables until tender.
3. Add garlic, ginger, soy sauce, and teriyaki sauce. Cook for 1-2 minutes.
4. Return beef to the pan and toss everything together. Serve over rice.

Shepherd's Pie

Ingredients

- 1 lb (450 g) ground beef
- 2 cups mashed potatoes
- 1 cup frozen peas and carrots
- 1 medium onion, diced
- 2 cloves garlic, minced
- 1/4 cup beef broth
- 2 tbsp tomato paste
- 1 tsp Worcestershire sauce
- Salt and pepper, to taste

Instructions

1. Brown ground beef with onion and garlic in a skillet. Stir in tomato paste, Worcestershire sauce, and beef broth.
2. Add frozen vegetables and cook until tender. Season with salt and pepper.
3. Transfer mixture to a baking dish and top with mashed potatoes.
4. Bake at 375°F (190°C) for 20 minutes, or until top is golden.

Beef Potstickers

Ingredients

- 1 lb (450 g) ground beef
- 1/2 cup cabbage, finely chopped
- 2 green onions, chopped
- 1 tbsp soy sauce
- 1 tbsp sesame oil
- 1/2 tsp garlic, minced
- 1 package dumpling wrappers
- Vegetable oil, for frying

Instructions

1. Combine beef, cabbage, green onions, soy sauce, sesame oil, and garlic.
2. Place 1 tbsp of mixture in the center of each wrapper, fold, and seal.
3. Heat oil in a skillet and fry potstickers until golden on both sides.
4. Add a splash of water and cover to steam for 5 minutes.

Beef Nachos Supreme

Ingredients

- 1 lb (450 g) ground beef
- 1 bag tortilla chips
- 1 cup shredded cheddar cheese
- 1/2 cup sour cream
- 1/2 cup salsa
- 1/4 cup jalapeños, sliced
- 1/4 cup green onions, chopped

Instructions

1. Cook ground beef with your choice of taco seasoning.
2. Spread tortilla chips on a baking sheet and top with beef and cheese.
3. Bake at 375°F (190°C) for 10-12 minutes until cheese is melted.
4. Top with sour cream, salsa, jalapeños, and green onions.

Beef Quesadillas

Ingredients

- 1 lb (450 g) ground beef
- 1 packet taco seasoning
- 4 flour tortillas
- 1 cup shredded cheese
- 1/2 cup salsa

Instructions

1. Brown beef and add taco seasoning.
2. Place beef and cheese on tortillas, fold, and cook in a skillet until golden brown on both sides.
3. Slice and serve with salsa.

Slow-Cooked Beef Ragu

Ingredients

- 1 lb (450 g) beef chuck roast
- 1 can (15 oz) crushed tomatoes
- 1 onion, chopped
- 2 cloves garlic, minced
- 1 cup beef broth
- 1 tsp dried oregano
- 1 tsp basil
- 2 tbsp olive oil

Instructions

1. Brown beef in olive oil and transfer to a slow cooker.
2. Add tomatoes, onion, garlic, broth, and herbs.
3. Cook on low for 6-8 hours, then shred beef. Serve over pasta.

Beef and Sweet Potato Hash

Ingredients

- 1 lb (450 g) ground beef
- 2 medium sweet potatoes, diced
- 1/2 onion, diced
- 2 cloves garlic, minced
- 1 tsp smoked paprika
- 1 tsp cumin
- Salt and pepper, to taste
- 2 eggs (optional)

Instructions

1. Cook ground beef in a skillet and set aside.
2. In the same pan, sauté sweet potatoes, onion, and garlic until tender.
3. Add beef, paprika, cumin, salt, and pepper, and stir to combine.
4. Optionally, top with a fried egg and serve.

Chipotle Beef Tacos

Ingredients

- 1 lb (450 g) ground beef
- 2 tbsp chipotle chili powder
- 1 tsp cumin
- 1/2 tsp smoked paprika
- 1/2 tsp garlic powder
- 1/2 tsp onion powder
- 1/2 cup beef broth
- 1 tbsp lime juice
- 8 small corn or flour tortillas
- 1 cup shredded lettuce
- 1/2 cup diced tomatoes
- 1/2 cup sour cream
- 1/4 cup chopped fresh cilantro

Instructions

1. Brown ground beef in a skillet over medium heat.
2. Stir in chipotle chili powder, cumin, paprika, garlic powder, and onion powder.
3. Add beef broth and lime juice. Simmer for 5-7 minutes, until thickened.
4. Warm tortillas and fill with beef mixture. Top with lettuce, tomatoes, sour cream, and cilantro. Serve immediately.

Beef Wellington Bites

Ingredients

- 1 lb (450 g) beef tenderloin, cut into bite-sized pieces
- 1 package puff pastry, thawed
- 1/2 cup mushrooms, finely chopped
- 2 tbsp Dijon mustard
- 1/4 cup Parmesan cheese, grated
- 1 egg, beaten (for egg wash)
- Salt and pepper, to taste

Instructions

1. Sear beef pieces in a hot skillet until browned, about 2-3 minutes. Let cool and brush with Dijon mustard.
2. Sauté mushrooms until tender, then drain excess moisture.
3. Roll out puff pastry and cut into squares. Place a beef piece and mushroom mixture on each square.
4. Fold the pastry over and seal. Brush with egg wash and bake at 375°F (190°C) for 15-20 minutes, or until golden brown.

Beef Meatball Subs

Ingredients

- 1 lb (450 g) ground beef
- 1/4 cup breadcrumbs
- 1/4 cup Parmesan cheese, grated
- 1 egg
- 2 cloves garlic, minced
- 1/2 tsp dried oregano
- 1/2 tsp dried basil
- 1 jar marinara sauce
- 4 sub rolls
- 1 cup shredded mozzarella cheese

Instructions

1. Mix ground beef, breadcrumbs, Parmesan, egg, garlic, oregano, and basil. Shape into meatballs.
2. Brown meatballs in a skillet, then add marinara sauce. Simmer for 10 minutes.
3. Place meatballs in sub rolls, top with sauce and mozzarella.
4. Broil in the oven for 3-5 minutes, until cheese is melted.

Chimichurri Steak Salad

Ingredients

- 1 lb (450 g) flank steak
- 2 cups mixed salad greens
- 1/2 red onion, thinly sliced
- 1/2 cup cherry tomatoes, halved
- 1/4 cup fresh cilantro, chopped
- 1/4 cup fresh parsley, chopped
- 1 tbsp red wine vinegar
- 1/2 cup olive oil
- 2 cloves garlic, minced
- 1 tsp red pepper flakes
- Salt and pepper, to taste

Instructions

1. Grill or sear flank steak to desired doneness. Let rest, then slice thinly against the grain.
2. For the chimichurri, whisk together red wine vinegar, olive oil, garlic, cilantro, parsley, red pepper flakes, salt, and pepper.
3. Toss salad greens, onion, tomatoes, and steak with chimichurri sauce. Serve immediately.

Beef Stuffed Bell Peppers

Ingredients

- 1 lb (450 g) ground beef
- 4 large bell peppers, tops cut off and seeds removed
- 1 cup cooked rice
- 1 can (14.5 oz) diced tomatoes
- 1 tsp dried oregano
- 1/2 tsp garlic powder
- 1/2 tsp onion powder
- 1/2 cup shredded cheese (cheddar or Mexican blend)
- Salt and pepper, to taste

Instructions

1. Brown ground beef in a skillet, then stir in diced tomatoes, rice, oregano, garlic powder, onion powder, salt, and pepper.
2. Stuff bell peppers with the beef mixture.
3. Place peppers in a baking dish and top with cheese. Bake at 375°F (190°C) for 25-30 minutes, until peppers are tender.

Moroccan Spiced Beef Stew

Ingredients

- 1 lb (450 g) beef stew meat, cubed
- 1 onion, diced
- 2 carrots, chopped
- 2 cloves garlic, minced
- 1 can (14.5 oz) diced tomatoes
- 4 cups beef broth
- 1 tsp cumin
- 1 tsp coriander
- 1/2 tsp cinnamon
- 1/2 tsp turmeric
- 1/4 tsp cayenne pepper (optional)
- Salt and pepper, to taste

Instructions

1. Brown beef stew meat in a pot, then set aside.
2. In the same pot, sauté onion, carrots, and garlic until softened.
3. Stir in spices, tomatoes, and beef broth. Bring to a boil, then reduce heat and simmer for 1-2 hours until beef is tender.
4. Season with salt and pepper and serve.

Beef Lasagna Rolls

Ingredients

- 1 lb (450 g) ground beef
- 9 lasagna noodles, cooked
- 1 jar (24 oz) marinara sauce
- 1 cup ricotta cheese
- 1 1/2 cups shredded mozzarella cheese
- 1/4 cup grated Parmesan cheese
- 1 egg
- 1 tsp dried basil
- 1/2 tsp garlic powder
- Salt and pepper, to taste

Instructions

1. Brown ground beef in a skillet, then stir in marinara sauce and simmer for 10 minutes.
2. In a bowl, combine ricotta, mozzarella, Parmesan, egg, basil, garlic powder, salt, and pepper.
3. Spread ricotta mixture on lasagna noodles, then roll them up.
4. Place rolls in a baking dish, cover with sauce, and bake at 375°F (190°C) for 25-30 minutes, until bubbly.

Beef Curry with Rice

Ingredients

- 1 lb (450 g) beef stew meat, cubed
- 2 tbsp curry powder
- 1 can (14 oz) coconut milk
- 1 onion, diced
- 1 carrot, chopped
- 2 cloves garlic, minced
- 2 tbsp vegetable oil
- 1 1/2 cups beef broth
- Salt and pepper, to taste
- Cooked rice, for serving

Instructions

1. Brown beef in a pot with vegetable oil.
2. Add onion, carrot, and garlic, and cook until softened.
3. Stir in curry powder, coconut milk, beef broth, salt, and pepper.
4. Simmer for 1-1.5 hours until beef is tender. Serve over rice.

Roast Beef Sandwiches

Ingredients

- 1 lb (450 g) roast beef, sliced
- 4 sandwich rolls
- 1/4 cup horseradish sauce
- 1/4 cup mayonnaise
- 1/4 cup shredded lettuce
- 1/4 cup sliced pickles

Instructions

1. Toast sandwich rolls and spread horseradish sauce on one side and mayonnaise on the other.
2. Layer roast beef, lettuce, and pickles.
3. Close sandwiches and serve.

Beef and Spinach Quiche

Ingredients

- 1 lb (450 g) ground beef
- 1 cup spinach, chopped
- 1/2 cup shredded cheese (cheddar or mozzarella)
- 1 pie crust
- 4 eggs
- 1/2 cup milk
- Salt and pepper, to taste

Instructions

1. Brown ground beef in a skillet, then stir in spinach and cook until wilted.
2. In a bowl, whisk eggs, milk, salt, and pepper.
3. Layer beef and spinach mixture in the pie crust, then pour egg mixture over the top.
4. Sprinkle with cheese and bake at 375°F (190°C) for 30-35 minutes, or until set.

Beef Lettuce Wraps

Ingredients

- 1 lb (450 g) ground beef
- 1 tbsp soy sauce
- 1 tbsp hoisin sauce
- 1 tbsp rice vinegar
- 1 tsp sesame oil
- 2 cloves garlic, minced
- 1/2 onion, finely chopped
- 1/2 cup shredded carrots
- 1/4 cup chopped green onions
- 1/4 cup chopped fresh cilantro
- 8-10 large lettuce leaves (such as iceberg or butter lettuce)
- 1 tbsp sesame seeds (optional)

Instructions

1. Heat sesame oil in a skillet over medium heat. Add garlic and onion, cooking until softened.
2. Add ground beef and cook, breaking it up, until browned.
3. Stir in soy sauce, hoisin sauce, rice vinegar, and shredded carrots. Cook for 2-3 minutes until well combined.
4. Spoon beef mixture into lettuce leaves, topping with green onions, cilantro, and sesame seeds. Serve immediately.

Mongolian Beef with Rice

Ingredients

- 1 lb (450 g) flank steak, thinly sliced
- 2 tbsp soy sauce
- 2 tbsp hoisin sauce
- 1 tbsp brown sugar
- 1/2 tsp garlic powder
- 1/2 tsp ground ginger
- 2 tbsp vegetable oil
- 1/2 cup green onions, chopped
- 1 cup cooked rice

Instructions

1. In a small bowl, whisk together soy sauce, hoisin sauce, brown sugar, garlic powder, and ginger.
2. Heat vegetable oil in a skillet over medium-high heat. Add sliced steak and cook until browned.
3. Add the sauce mixture and green onions, cooking for another 2-3 minutes until the sauce thickens.
4. Serve over cooked rice and garnish with extra green onions.

Beef and Cheese Empanadas

Ingredients

- 1 lb (450 g) ground beef
- 1 small onion, chopped
- 1/2 cup green olives, chopped
- 1/4 cup raisins
- 1 tsp cumin
- 1/2 tsp paprika
- 1/4 tsp cayenne pepper (optional)
- 1 cup shredded cheese (cheddar or mozzarella)
- 1 package empanada dough discs (10-12)
- 1 egg, beaten (for egg wash)

Instructions

1. Brown ground beef in a skillet over medium heat. Add chopped onion, olives, raisins, cumin, paprika, and cayenne. Cook until the onion softens.
2. Stir in shredded cheese and let cool.
3. Place a spoonful of the beef mixture onto each empanada disc. Fold and seal the edges.
4. Brush with beaten egg and bake at 375°F (190°C) for 20-25 minutes, until golden brown.

Shredded Beef Tostadas

Ingredients

- 1 lb (450 g) beef chuck roast
- 1 onion, quartered
- 2 cloves garlic, smashed
- 1 can (14.5 oz) diced tomatoes
- 1 tsp ground cumin
- 1 tsp chili powder
- 1/2 tsp oregano
- 8 tostada shells
- 1/2 cup shredded lettuce
- 1/2 cup diced tomatoes
- 1/4 cup sour cream
- 1/4 cup chopped fresh cilantro

Instructions

1. In a slow cooker, add beef, onion, garlic, diced tomatoes, cumin, chili powder, and oregano. Cook on low for 6-8 hours until the beef is tender.
2. Shred the beef with a fork.
3. Assemble tostadas by layering shredded beef, lettuce, tomatoes, sour cream, and cilantro on each shell. Serve immediately.

Beef Sloppy Joes

Ingredients

- 1 lb (450 g) ground beef
- 1/2 onion, chopped
- 1/2 bell pepper, chopped
- 2 cloves garlic, minced
- 1 can (8 oz) tomato sauce
- 1 tbsp brown sugar
- 1 tbsp Worcestershire sauce
- 1 tbsp mustard
- 1 tsp chili powder
- 4 hamburger buns

Instructions

1. Brown ground beef in a skillet over medium heat. Add onion, bell pepper, and garlic, cooking until softened.
2. Stir in tomato sauce, brown sugar, Worcestershire sauce, mustard, and chili powder.
3. Simmer for 5-7 minutes until the mixture thickens.
4. Spoon the sloppy joe mixture onto buns and serve immediately.

Beef Pad Thai

Ingredients

- 1 lb (450 g) flank steak or sirloin, thinly sliced
- 8 oz rice noodles
- 2 tbsp soy sauce
- 1 tbsp fish sauce
- 1 tbsp lime juice
- 1 tbsp brown sugar
- 2 cloves garlic, minced
- 1 egg, lightly beaten
- 1/4 cup chopped peanuts
- 1/4 cup chopped cilantro
- 1/4 cup bean sprouts (optional)
- 1 lime, cut into wedges

Instructions

1. Cook rice noodles according to package instructions. Set aside.
2. In a skillet, heat oil over medium-high heat. Add sliced beef and cook until browned.
3. Push beef to one side of the pan and scramble the egg on the other side.
4. Stir in garlic, soy sauce, fish sauce, lime juice, brown sugar, and cooked noodles. Toss to combine.
5. Garnish with peanuts, cilantro, bean sprouts, and lime wedges. Serve immediately.

Grilled Steak and Asparagus Salad

Ingredients

- 1 lb (450 g) flank steak or sirloin
- 1 bunch asparagus, trimmed
- 4 cups mixed salad greens
- 1/2 cup cherry tomatoes, halved
- 1/4 cup blue cheese crumbles (optional)
- 1/4 cup balsamic vinaigrette

Instructions

1. Grill steak to your desired doneness and let rest before slicing thinly.
2. Grill asparagus for 3-4 minutes until tender.
3. Toss salad greens, cherry tomatoes, and asparagus in a bowl.
4. Top with sliced steak and blue cheese. Drizzle with balsamic vinaigrette and serve immediately.

Beef Burrito Enchiladas

Ingredients

- 1 lb (450 g) ground beef
- 1 can (10 oz) enchilada sauce
- 1 cup shredded cheese (cheddar or Mexican blend)
- 8 flour tortillas
- 1/2 cup sour cream
- 1/4 cup chopped fresh cilantro

Instructions

1. Brown ground beef in a skillet. Stir in half of the enchilada sauce and simmer for 5 minutes.
2. Spoon beef mixture onto tortillas and roll them up.
3. Place rolled tortillas in a baking dish and pour remaining enchilada sauce over them. Top with cheese.
4. Bake at 375°F (190°C) for 20 minutes or until cheese is melted and bubbly. Serve with sour cream and cilantro.

Spicy Beef Stir-Fry with Noodles

Ingredients

- 1 lb (450 g) beef sirloin, thinly sliced
- 8 oz noodles (rice or egg noodles)
- 1 red bell pepper, sliced
- 1 carrot, julienned
- 2 tbsp soy sauce
- 2 tbsp hoisin sauce
- 1 tbsp sriracha sauce (adjust to taste)
- 1 tbsp sesame oil
- 2 cloves garlic, minced
- 1/4 cup chopped green onions

Instructions

1. Cook noodles according to package instructions and set aside.
2. In a wok or skillet, heat sesame oil over medium-high heat. Stir-fry beef until browned, then set aside.
3. In the same skillet, stir-fry bell pepper, carrot, and garlic for 2-3 minutes.
4. Add beef, noodles, soy sauce, hoisin sauce, and sriracha. Toss to combine and heat through.
5. Garnish with green onions and serve immediately.

Beef and Black Bean Chili

Ingredients

- 1 lb (450 g) ground beef
- 1 onion, chopped
- 1 can (15 oz) black beans, drained and rinsed
- 1 can (14.5 oz) diced tomatoes
- 1 can (6 oz) tomato paste
- 1 tbsp chili powder
- 1 tsp cumin
- 1/2 tsp smoked paprika
- 1/2 tsp oregano
- Salt and pepper, to taste

Instructions

1. Brown ground beef in a pot over medium heat. Add onion and cook until softened.
2. Stir in black beans, diced tomatoes, tomato paste, chili powder, cumin, paprika, oregano, salt, and pepper.
3. Simmer for 30-40 minutes, stirring occasionally, until the chili thickens.
4. Serve with toppings like sour cream, shredded cheese, and cilantro.

Mediterranean Beef Pita Wraps

Ingredients

- 1 lb (450 g) ground beef
- 1 tbsp olive oil
- 1 onion, finely chopped
- 2 cloves garlic, minced
- 1 tsp ground cumin
- 1 tsp dried oregano
- 1/2 tsp cinnamon
- 1/4 tsp ground allspice
- Salt and pepper, to taste
- 4 pita bread pockets
- 1 cup chopped cucumber
- 1 cup diced tomatoes
- 1/4 cup crumbled feta cheese
- 1/4 cup chopped fresh parsley
- 1/4 cup tzatziki sauce (optional)

Instructions

1. Heat olive oil in a skillet over medium heat. Add onion and garlic, cooking until softened.
2. Add ground beef, cumin, oregano, cinnamon, allspice, salt, and pepper. Cook, breaking up the beef, until browned.
3. Toast pita pockets until warm and slightly crispy.
4. Stuff each pita with the beef mixture, cucumber, tomato, feta, and parsley. Drizzle with tzatziki sauce if desired. Serve immediately.

Steak Tacos with Lime Crema

Ingredients

- 1 lb (450 g) flank steak
- 2 tbsp olive oil
- 1 tsp chili powder
- 1 tsp cumin
- 1/2 tsp garlic powder
- 1/4 tsp smoked paprika
- Salt and pepper, to taste
- 8 small tortillas
- 1/2 cup sour cream
- 1 tbsp lime juice
- 1 tbsp chopped fresh cilantro
- 1/2 cup diced onion
- 1/2 cup chopped cilantro (for garnish)

Instructions

1. Rub flank steak with olive oil, chili powder, cumin, garlic powder, smoked paprika, salt, and pepper.
2. Grill steak to desired doneness (about 5-7 minutes per side for medium). Let rest for 5 minutes before slicing thinly against the grain.
3. In a small bowl, mix sour cream, lime juice, and chopped cilantro to make the lime crema.
4. Warm tortillas in a dry skillet.
5. Assemble tacos with steak slices, onion, and cilantro. Top with a dollop of lime crema and serve.

Classic Beef Burger

Ingredients

- 1 lb (450 g) ground beef (80% lean)
- Salt and pepper, to taste
- 4 hamburger buns
- 4 slices cheddar cheese
- Lettuce, tomato, and onion slices, for topping
- Ketchup and mustard (optional)

Instructions

1. Preheat grill or skillet over medium-high heat.
2. Form ground beef into 4 patties and season with salt and pepper.
3. Grill or cook patties for 4-5 minutes per side, until desired doneness is achieved. Add a slice of cheese during the last minute of cooking.
4. Toast the buns lightly on the grill or in a skillet.
5. Assemble burgers with cheese, lettuce, tomato, onion, and condiments. Serve immediately.

Beef and Barley Soup

Ingredients

- 1 lb (450 g) stew beef, cut into cubes
- 1 tbsp olive oil
- 1 onion, chopped
- 2 carrots, peeled and chopped
- 2 celery stalks, chopped
- 2 cloves garlic, minced
- 1 cup barley
- 6 cups beef broth
- 1 can (14.5 oz) diced tomatoes
- 1 tsp dried thyme
- 1/2 tsp ground black pepper
- Salt, to taste

Instructions

1. Heat olive oil in a large pot. Add stew beef and brown on all sides.
2. Add onion, carrots, celery, and garlic, cooking for 5-6 minutes until softened.
3. Stir in barley, beef broth, diced tomatoes, thyme, pepper, and salt. Bring to a boil.
4. Reduce heat, cover, and simmer for 1-1.5 hours, until barley is tender and beef is fully cooked. Serve hot.

Steak and Potato Salad

Ingredients

- 1 lb (450 g) steak (sirloin or ribeye)
- 4 medium potatoes, boiled and cubed
- 1/4 cup olive oil
- 2 tbsp balsamic vinegar
- 1 tbsp Dijon mustard
- 1/4 tsp garlic powder
- Salt and pepper, to taste
- 2 cups mixed salad greens
- 1/2 red onion, thinly sliced
- 1/4 cup crumbled blue cheese (optional)

Instructions

1. Grill or pan-sear steak to desired doneness. Let rest before slicing thinly.
2. Whisk together olive oil, balsamic vinegar, Dijon mustard, garlic powder, salt, and pepper.
3. In a large bowl, toss salad greens, potatoes, red onion, and blue cheese.
4. Drizzle with the dressing and top with sliced steak. Serve immediately.

Beef Picadillo

Ingredients

- 1 lb (450 g) ground beef
- 1 onion, chopped
- 2 cloves garlic, minced
- 1/2 cup green olives, chopped
- 1/4 cup raisins
- 1/2 cup diced potatoes
- 1 tsp ground cumin
- 1 tsp ground cinnamon
- 1/2 tsp oregano
- 1 tbsp tomato paste
- 1 can (14.5 oz) diced tomatoes
- 1/4 cup chopped fresh cilantro

Instructions

1. In a skillet, brown ground beef over medium heat. Drain excess fat.
2. Add onion, garlic, olives, raisins, and diced potatoes. Cook for 5 minutes.
3. Stir in cumin, cinnamon, oregano, tomato paste, and diced tomatoes. Simmer for 15-20 minutes until potatoes are tender.
4. Garnish with cilantro and serve with rice.

Italian Beef Paninis

Ingredients

- 1 lb (450 g) thinly sliced roast beef
- 4 ciabatta rolls
- 1/2 cup marinara sauce
- 1/2 cup mozzarella cheese, shredded
- 1/4 cup Parmesan cheese, grated
- 1 tbsp olive oil
- 1/2 tsp garlic powder
- Fresh basil leaves

Instructions

1. Preheat a panini press or grill pan.
2. Cut ciabatta rolls in half. Spread marinara sauce on the bottom half of each roll.
3. Layer with sliced roast beef, mozzarella, Parmesan, and fresh basil.
4. Top with the other half of the roll. Brush the outsides with olive oil and sprinkle with garlic powder.
5. Grill in the panini press for 4-5 minutes until crispy and golden. Serve warm.

Beef Fried Rice

Ingredients

- 1 lb (450 g) ground beef
- 2 cups cooked rice (preferably day-old)
- 1/2 onion, chopped
- 2 cloves garlic, minced
- 2 eggs, scrambled
- 1/2 cup frozen peas and carrots
- 2 tbsp soy sauce
- 1 tbsp sesame oil
- 1 tsp ginger, grated
- 2 green onions, chopped

Instructions

1. In a large skillet or wok, cook ground beef over medium heat until browned.
2. Add onion and garlic, cooking until softened.
3. Stir in scrambled eggs, peas, carrots, and cooked rice.
4. Season with soy sauce, sesame oil, and ginger. Stir well.
5. Garnish with green onions and serve hot.

www.ingramcontent.com/pod-product-compliance
Lightning Source LLC
LaVergne TN
LVHW081323060526
838201LV00055B/2427